Easy Air Fryer Cookbook

Easy and Tasty Low-Fat Recipes to Cook with Your Air Fryer on a Budget

Linda Wang

© **Copyright 2021 by Linda Wang - All rights reserved.**

The content contained within this book may not be reproduced, duplicated or transmitted without direct written permission from the author or the publisher.
Under no circumstances will any blame or legal responsibility be held against the publisher, or author, for any damages, reparation, or monetary loss due to the information contained within this book. Either directly or indirectly.

Legal Notice:
This book is copyright protected. This book is only for personal use. You cannot amend, distribute, sell, use, quote or paraphrase any part, or the content within this book, without the consent of the author or publisher.

Disclaimer Notice:
Please note the information contained within this document is for educational and entertainment purposes only. All effort has been executed to present accurate, up to date, and reliable, complete information. No warranties of any kind are declared or implied. Readers acknowledge that the author is not engaging in the rendering of legal, financial, medical or professional advice. The content within this book has been derived from various sources. Please consult a licensed professional before attempting any techniques outlined in this book.
By reading this document, the reader agrees that under no circumstances is the author responsible for any losses, direct or indirect, which are incurred as a result of the use of information contained within this document, including, but not limited to, — errors, omissions, or inaccuracies.

TABLE OF CONTENTS

INTRODUCTION 1

Mushroom Leek Frittata 5

Crispy Ham Egg Cups 7

Ham and Egg Toast Cups 9

Cauliflower Hash Brown 11

Egg Veggie Frittata 13

Stuffed Potato Recipe 15

Smoked Bacon and Bread 17

Cod Tortilla 19

Herbed Tomatoes 21

Okra Casserole 23

Eggplant and Leeks Stew 25

Peppers and Tomatoes Mix 27

Zucchini Spaghetti 28

Roasted Tomatoes 30

Special Potatoes Side Dish 32

Parmesan Cheese Salmon 34

Miso Fish 36

Garlic Parmesan Shrimp 37

Butter Trout 39

Ginger Cod Steaks 41

Salmon Patties 43

Pea Pods and Shrimp Mix 45

Chicken with Cacciatore (Chicken Hunter) 46

Sweet Sriracha Turkey Legs 48

Turkey with Fig Sauce 50

Chicken and Chickpeas 52

Cumin Chicken Wings 54

Chicken Sandwich 56

Herbed Pork Burgers 58

Garlic Butter Pork Chops 60

Jalapeno Beef 62

Marinated Beef 64

Roast Pork with Vegetables 65

Almond Asparagus 67

Crispy Marinated Tofu 69

Lemon Rice Soup 71

Coconut Lime Soup 73

Spiced Butternut Squash (Vegan) 75

Herbed Potatoes (Vegan) 77

Spicy Potatoes (Vegan) 79

Bow Tie Pasta Chips 81

Buttered Dinner Rolls 83

Baked Egg Plant with Bacon 85

Walnut and Vanilla Bars 87

Currant Cookies 89

Fried Banana Slices 91

Creamy Blackberry 93

Pineapple and Carrot Cake 94

Maple Cinnamon Buns 96

Bread Pudding with Cranberry 99

NOTES 101

INTRODUCTION

An Air Fryer is a magic revolutionized kitchen appliance that helps you fry with less or even no oil at all. This kind of product applies Rapid Air technology, which offers a new way to fry with less oil. This new invention cooks food through the circulation of superheated air and generates 80% low-fat food. Although the food is fried with less oil, you don't need to worry as the food processed by the Air Fryer still has the same taste like the food fried using the deep-frying method.

This technology uses a superheated element, which radiates heat close to the food and an exhaust fan in its lid to circulate airflow. An Air Fryer ensures that the food processed is cooked completely. The exhaust fan located at the top of the cooking chamber helps the food get the same heating temperature in every part quickly, resulting in a cooked food of better and healthier quality. Besides, cooking with an Air Fryer is also suitable for those individuals which are too busy or do not have enough time. For example, an Air Fryer only needs half a spoonful of oil and takes 10 minutes to serve a medium bowl of crispy French fries.

In addition to serving healthier food, an Air Fryer also provides some other benefits to you. Since an Air Fryer helps you fry using less oil or without oil for some kind of food, it automatically reduces the fat and cholesterol content in food. Indeed, no one will refuse to enjoy fried food without worrying about the greasy and fat content. Having fried food with no guilt is one of the pleasures of life. Besides having low fat and cholesterol, you save some amount of money by consuming oil sparingly, which can be used for other needs. An Air Fryer also can reheat your food. Sometimes, when you have fried leftover and you reheat it, it will usually serve reheated greasy food with some addition of unhealthy reuse oil. Undoubtedly, the saturated fat in the fried food gets worse because of this process. An Air Fryer helps you reheat your food without being afraid of extra oils that the food may absorb. Fried bananas, fish and chips, nuggets, or even fried chicken can be reheated to become as warm and crispy as they were before by using an Air Fryer.

Some people may think that spending some amount of money to buy a fryer is wasteful. I dare to say that they are wrong because an Air Fryer is not only used to fry. It is a sophisticated multi-function appliance since it also helps you to roast chicken, make steak, grill fish, and even bake a cake. With a built-in air filter, an Air Fryer filters the air and saves your kitchen from smoke and grease.

An air Fryer is really a new innovative method of cooking. Grab it fast and welcome to a clean and healthy kitchen.

Mushroom Leek Frittata

Preparation Time: 10 minutes

Cooking Time: 32 minutes

Serve: 4

Ingredients:

- 6 oz mushrooms, sliced
- 6 eggs
- 1 cup leeks, sliced
- Salt

Directions:

1. Preheat the air fryer to 325 degrees F.
2. Spray air fryer baking dish with cooking spray and set aside.
3. Heat another pan over medium heat. Spray pan with cooking spray.
4. Add mushrooms, leeks, and salt in a pan sauté for 6 minutes.
5. Break eggs in a bowl and whisk well.

6. Transfer sautéed mushroom and leek mixture into the prepared baking dish.
7. Pour egg over mushroom mixture.
8. Place dish in the air fryer and cook for 32 minutes.
9. Serve and enjoy.

Nutrition:

Calories 116, Fat 7 g, Carbohydrates 5.1 g, Sugar 2.1 g, Protein 10 g, Cholesterol 245 mg

Crispy Ham Egg Cups

Preparation Time: 17 minutes

Servings: 2

Ingredients:

- 4 large eggs.
- 4: 1-oz.slices deli ham

- ¼ cup diced green bell pepper.
- ½ cup shredded medium Cheddar cheese.
- 2 tbsp. diced red bell pepper.
- 2 tbsp. full-fat sour cream.
- 2 tbsp. diced white onion.

Directions:

1. Place one slice of ham on the bottom of four baking cups.
2. Take a large bowl, whisk eggs with sour cream. Stir in green pepper, red pepper and onion
3. Pour the egg mixture into ham-lined baking cups. Top with Cheddar. Place cups into the air fryer basket. Adjust the temperature to 320 Degrees F and set the timer for 12 minutes or until the tops are browned. Serve warm.

Nutrition:

Calories: 382; Protein: 29.4g; Fiber: 1.4g; Fat: 23.6g; Carbs: 6.0g

Ham and Egg Toast Cups

Preparation Time: 5 minutes

Cooking Time: 5 minutes

Servings: 2

Ingredients:
- 2 eggs
- 2 tablespoons butter
- 2 slices of ham

- Cheddar cheese, for topping
- Black pepper, to taste
- Salt, to taste

Directions:

1. Preheat the Air fryer to 400 degrees F and grease both ramekins with melted butter.
2. Place each ham slice in the greased ramekins and crack each egg over ham slices.
3. Sprinkle with salt, black pepper and cheddar cheese and transfer into the Air fryer basket.
4. Cook for about 5 minutes and remove the ramekins from the basket.
5. Serve warm.

Nutrition:

Calories: 202, Fat: 13.7g, Carbs: 7.4g, Sugar: 3.3g, Protein: 10.2g, Sodium: 203mg

Cauliflower Hash Brown

Preparation Time: 20 minutes

Cooking Time: 10 minutes

Servings: 4

Ingredients:

- 2 tablespoons xanthan gum
- 2 cups cauliflower, finely grated, soaked and drained
- Pepper powder, to taste
- 2 teaspoons chili flakes
- 1 teaspoon garlic
- 1 teaspoon onion powder
- 2 teaspoons vegetable oil
- Salt, to taste

Directions:

1. Preheat the Air fryer to 300 degrees F and grease an Air fryer basket with oil.
2. Heat vegetable oil in a nonstick pan and add cauliflower.

3. Sauté for about 4 minutes and dish out the cauliflower in a plate.
4. Mix the cauliflower with xanthum gum, salt, chili flakes, garlic and onion powder.
5. Mix well and refrigerate the hash for about 20 minutes.
6. Place the hash in the Air fryer basket and cook for about 10 minutes.
7. Flip the hash after cooking halfway through and dish out to serve warm.

Nutrition:

Calories: 291, Fat: 2.8g, Carbs: 6.5g, Sugar: 4.5g, Protein: 6.6g, Sodium: 62mg

Egg Veggie Frittata

Preparation Time: 10 minutes

Cooking Time: 18 minutes

Servings: 2

Ingredients:

- 4 eggs
- ½ cup milk
- 2 green onions, chopped

- ¼ cup spinach, chopped
- ¼ cup baby Bella mushrooms, chopped
- ½ teaspoon salt
- ½ teaspoon black pepper
- Dash of hot sauce

Directions:

1. Preheat the Air fryer to 365°F and grease 6x3 inch square pan with butter.
2. Whisk eggs with milk in a large bowl and stir in green onions, mushrooms and spinach.
3. Sprinkle with salt, black pepper and hot sauce and pour this mixture into the prepared pan.
4. Place in the Air fryer and cook for about 18 minutes.
5. Dish out in a platter and serve warm.

Nutrition:

Calories: 166, Fat: 10.1g, Carbohydrates: 5.8g, Sugar: 4g, Protein: 13.8g, Sodium: 748mg

Stuffed Potato Recipe

Preparation time: 20 minutes;

Cooking time: 14 minutes;

Serve: 4

Ingredients:

- Ham
- 150g Potatoes
- Cheese
- Olive oil

- Garlic powder
- Salt

Direction:

1. Cut your potato into strips but don't get to the end.
2. Paint your potato with a little oil so that it doesn't burn.
3. Add salt and pepper.
4. Put the potato 35 minutes at 180ºC without preheating.
5. Fill each cut with ham and cheese to taste.
6. Put the potato back 10 minutes more at 180 ºC.

Nutrition:

Calories 379.6, Fat 17.6 g, Carbohydrate 40.7 g, Sugars 4.0 g, Protein 14.0 g, Cholesterol 25.4 mg

Smoked Bacon and Bread

Preparation Time: 40 minutes

Servings: 6

Ingredients:

- 1 lb. white bread; cubed
- 1/2 lb. cheddar cheese; shredded
- 1 lb. smoked bacon; cooked and chopped.
- 1/2 lb. Monterey jack cheese; shredded

- 30 oz. canned tomatoes; chopped.
- 1 red onion; chopped.
- 1/4 cup avocado oil
- 2 tbsp. chicken stock
- 2 tbsp. chives; chopped.
- 8 eggs; whisked
- Salt and black pepper to taste

Directions:

1. Add the oil to your air fryer and heat it up at 350 °F
2. Add all other ingredients except the chives and cook for 30 minutes, shaking halfway. Divide between plates and serve with chives sprinkled on top

Cod Tortilla

Preparation Time: 27 minutes

Servings: 4

Ingredients:

- 4 cod fillets; skinless and boneless
- 4 tortillas
- 1 red onion; chopped.
- 1 green bell pepper; chopped.
- 1 cup corn
- A drizzle of olive oil
- 1/2 cup salsa
- 4 tbsp. parmesan cheese; grated
- A handful of baby spinach

Directions:

1. Put the fish fillets in your air fryer's basket, cook at 350 °F for 6 minutes and transfer to a plate.
2. Heat up a pan with the oil over medium heat, add the bell peppers, onions and corn and stir
3. Sauté for 5 minutes and take off the heat.

Arrange all the tortillas on a working surface and divide the cod, salsa, sautéed veggies, spinach and parmesan evenly between the 4 tortillas; then wrap / roll them

4. Place the tortillas in your air fryer's basket and cook at 350°F for 6 minutes. Divide between plates, serve.

Herbed Tomatoes

Preparation Time: 10 minutes

Cooking time: 20 minutes

Servings: 4

Ingredients:

- 1 pound tomatoes, cut into wedges
- 1 tablespoon oregano, chopped
- 2 tablespoons chives, chopped
- 1 tablespoon balsamic vinegar
- 1 teaspoon Italian seasoning
- A pinch of salt and black pepper
- 2 tablespoons olive oil

Directions:

1. In your air fryer's basket, combine the tomatoes with the chives, vinegar and the other ingredients, toss and cook at 360 degrees F for 20 minutes.
2. Divide everything between plates and serve as a side dish.

Nutrition:

Calories 89, fat 7, fiber 9, carbs 4, protein 2

Okra Casserole

Preparation Time: 25 minutes

Servings: 4

Ingredients:

- 2 tomatoes; chopped.
- 2 red bell peppers; cubed
- 3 cups okra
- 3 garlic cloves; minced
- ½ cup cheddar; shredded
- ¼ cup tomato puree
- 1 tbsp. cilantro; chopped.
- 1 tsp. olive oil
- 2 tsp. coriander, ground
- Salt and black pepper to taste.

Directions:

1. Grease a heat proof dish that fits your air fryer with the oil, add all the ingredients except the cilantro and the cheese and toss them really gently

2. Sprinkle the cheese and the cilantro on top, introduce the dish in the fryer and cook at 390 °F for 20 minutes.
3. Divide between plates and serve for lunch.

Nutrition:

Calories: 221; Fat: 7g; Fiber: 2g; Carbs: 4g; Protein: 9g

Eggplant and Leeks Stew

Preparation Time: 25 minutes

Servings: 4

Ingredients:

- 2 big eggplants, roughly cubed
- ½ bunch cilantro; chopped.

- 2 garlic cloves; minced
- 1 cup veggie stock
- 3 leeks; sliced
- 1 tbsp. hot sauce
- 2 tbsp. olive oil
- 1 tbsp. sweet paprika
- 1 tbsp. tomato puree
- Salt and black pepper to taste.

Directions:

1. In a pan that fits the air fryer, mix all the ingredients, toss, introduce in the fryer and cook at 380 °F for 20 minutes
2. Divide the stew into bowls and serve for lunch.

Nutrition:

Calories: 183; Fat: 4g; Fiber: 2g; Carbs: 4g; Protein: 12g

Peppers and Tomatoes Mix

Preparation Time: 5 minutes

Cooking time: 20 minutes

Servings: 4

Ingredients:

- 1 tablespoon olive oil
- 1 red onion, sliced
- 1 pound cherry tomatoes, halved
- 1 green bell pepper, cut in medium strips
- 1 red bell pepper, cut into medium strips
- 1 teaspoon chili powder
- 1 teaspoon garam masala
- Salt and black pepper to the taste

Directions:

1. In your air fryer, combine the tomatoes with the bell peppers and the other ingredients, toss and cook at 370 degrees F for 20 minutes.
2. Divide the mix between plates and serve as a side dish.

Nutrition:

Calories 172, fat 5, fiber 4, carbs 7, protein 4

Zucchini Spaghetti

Preparation Time: 20 minutes

Servings: 4

Ingredients:

- 1 lb. zucchinis, cut with a spiralizer
- ¼ cup parsley; chopped.
- 1 cup parmesan; grated
- 6 garlic cloves; minced
- ¼ cup olive oil
- ½ tsp. red pepper flakes

- Salt and black pepper to taste.

Directions:

1. In a pan that fits your air fryer, mix all the ingredients, toss, introduce in the fryer and cook at 370 °F for 15 minutes
2. Divide between plates and serve as a side dish.

Nutrition:

Calories: 200; Fat: 6g; Fiber: 3g; Carbs: 4g; Protein: 5g

Roasted Tomatoes

Preparation Time: 20 minutes

Servings: 4

Ingredients:

- 4 tomatoes; halved
- 1 tbsp. basil; chopped.
- ½ cup parmesan; grated
- ½ tsp. onion powder
- ½ tsp. oregano; dried

- ½ tsp. smoked paprika
- ½ tsp. garlic powder
- Cooking spray

Directions:

1. Take a bowl and mix all the ingredients except the cooking spray and the parmesan.
2. Arrange the tomatoes in your air fryer's pan, sprinkle the parmesan on top and grease with cooking spray
3. Cook at 370 °F for 15 minutes, divide between plates and serve.

Nutrition:

Calories: 200; Fat: 7g; Fiber: 2g; Carbs: 4g; Protein: 6g

Special Potatoes Side Dish

Preparation Time: 30 minutes

Servings: 2

Ingredients:

- 2 potatoes [medium]
- 3 tablespoon sour cream
- 1 teaspoon butter
- 1 teaspoon chives 1 teaspoon

- 1 ½ tablespoon cheese [grated]
- pepper according to taste
- salt according to taste

Directions:

1. Stab potatoes with fork and put in Air Fryer having boiled water so they are cooked from the inside to the outside properly.
2. Cook for 15 minutes at 350 degrees Fahrenheit.
3. In the meantime, mix sour cream, cheese and chives in a bowl. Cut open potatoes and spread butter and add toppings to them. Serve with raw salad.

Parmesan Cheese Salmon

Preparation Time: 10 minutes

Cooking Time: 16 minutes

Serve: 2

Ingredients:
- 2 salmon fillets
- 1/4 cup parmesan cheese, grated

  For pesto:
- 1/4 cup pine nuts
- 1/4 cup olive oil
- 1 1/2 cups fresh basil leaves
- 2 garlic cloves, peeled and chopped
- 1/4 cup parmesan cheese, grated
- 1/2 tsp pepper
- 1/2 tsp salt

Directions:
1. Add all pesto ingredients to the blender and blend until smooth.
2. Preheat the air fryer to 370 degrees F.

3. Spray air fryer basket with cooking spray.
4. Place salmon fillet into the air fryer basket and spread 2 tablespoons of the pesto on each salmon fillet.
5. Sprinkle grated cheese on top of the pesto.
6. Cook salmon for 16 minutes.
7. Serve and enjoy.

Nutrition:

Calories 725, Fat 57 g, Carbohydrates 4 g, Sugar 0.7 g, Protein 49 g, Cholesterol 108 mg

Miso Fish

Preparation Time: 10 minutes

Cooking Time: 10 minutes

Serve: 2

Ingredients:

- 2 cod fish fillets
- 1 tbsp garlic, chopped
- 2 tsp swerve
- 2 tbsp miso

Directions:

1. Add all ingredients to the zip-lock bag. Shake well place in the refrigerator for overnight.
2. Place marinated fish fillets into the air fryer basket and cook at 350 degrees F for 10 minutes.
3. Serve and enjoy.

Nutrition:

Calories 229, Fat 2.6 g, Carbohydrates 10.9 g, Sugar 6.1 g, Protein 43.4 g, Cholesterol 99 mg

Garlic Parmesan Shrimp

Preparation Time: 20 minutes

Cooking Time: 10 minutes

Servings: 2

Ingredients:

- 1 pound shrimp, deveined and peeled
- ¼ cup cilantro, diced
- ½ cup parmesan cheese, grated
- 1 tablespoon olive oil
- 1 teaspoon salt
- 1 teaspoon fresh cracked pepper
- 1 tablespoon lemon juice
- 6 garlic cloves, diced

Directions:

1. Preheat the Air fryer to 350 degrees F and grease an Air fryer basket.
2. Drizzle shrimp with olive oil and lemon juice and season with garlic, salt and cracked pepper.
3. Cover the bowl with plastic wrap and refrigerate

for about 3 hours.

4. Stir in the parmesan cheese and cilantro to the bowl and transfer to the Air fryer basket.
5. Cook for about 10 minutes and serve immediately.

Nutrition:

Calories: 602, Fat: 23.9g, Carbohydrates: 46.5g, Sugar: 2.9g, Protein: 11.3g, Sodium: 886mg

Butter Trout

Preparation Time: 22 minutes

Servings: 4

Ingredients:

- 4 trout fillets; boneless
- Juice of 1 lime
- 1 tbsp. parsley; chopped.

- 4 tbsp. butter; melted
- 1 tbsp. chives; chopped.
- Salt and black pepper to taste.

Directions:

1. Mix the fish fillets with the melted butter, salt and pepper, rub gently, put the fish in your air fryer's basket and cook at 390 °F for 6 minutes on each side.
2. Divide between plates and serve with lime juice drizzled on top and with parsley and chives sprinkled at the end.

Nutrition:

Calories: 221; Fat: 11g; Fiber: 4g; Carbs: 6g; Protein: 9g

Ginger Cod Steaks

Preparation time: 30 minutes

Servings: 2

Ingredients:

- Large cod steaks: 2 slices
- Ginger powder: .5 tsp.
- Turmeric powder: .25 tsp.
- Garlic powder: .5 tsp.
- Plum sauce: 1 tbsp.
- Ginger slices: as desired
- Salt & pepper: 1 pinch
- Kentucky Kernel Seasoned Flour: +Corn flour: 1 part of each

Directions:

1. Dry off the steaks and marinate using the pepper, salt, ginger powder, and turmeric powder for a few minutes.
2. Lightly coat the steaks with the corn flour/Kentucky mix.

3. Set the temperature in the fryer to 356º Fahrenheit for 15 minutes and increase to 400º Fahrenheit for 5 minutes.: Time may vary depending on the size of the cod.
4. Prepare the sauce in a wok. Brown the ginger slices and remove from the heat. Stir in the plum sauce adding water to thin as needed.
5. Serve the steaks with a drizzle of the prepared sauce.

Salmon Patties

Preparation time: 20 minutes

Servings: 6-8

Ingredients:

- Salmon fillet: 1 portion - approx. 7 oz.
- Russet potatoes: 3 large - approx. 14 oz.
- Frozen veggies: .33 cup
- Dill sprinkles: 2 pinches

- Salt and pepper: 1 dash each
- Egg: 1

Ingredients - The Coating:

- Breadcrumbs
- Olive oil spray

Directions:

1. Warm the Air Fryer to reach 356º Fahrenheit.
2. Peel and chop the potatoes into small bits. Boil for about ten minutes.
3. Mash and place in the refrigerator to cool.
4. Grill the salmon for five minutes. Flake it apart and set it aside for now.
5. Combine all of the fixings and shape into patties. Evenly coat with the breadcrumbs, and spray with a bit of olive oil spray.
6. Place in the fryer for 10-12 minutes.

Pea Pods and Shrimp Mix

Preparation Time: 18 minutes

Servings: 4

Ingredients:

- 1 lb. shrimp; peeled and deveined
- 3/4 cup pineapple juice
- 1/2 lb. pea pods
- 2 tbsp. soy sauce
- 3 tbsp. sugar
- 3 tbsp. balsamic vinegar

Directions:

1. In a pan that fits your air fryer, mix all the ingredients.
2. Place the pan in the fryer and cook at 380 °F for 8 minutes. Divide into bowls and serve

Chicken with Cacciatore (Chicken Hunter)

Preparation time: 10-20,

Cooking time: 30-45;

Serve: 6

Ingredients:

- 1 kg of chicken pieces
- 2 carrots
- 1 onion
- 3 celery stalks
- 1 clove garlic
- 400 g peeled tomatoes
- 1 glass of red wine
- 50 g of olives
- Salt, pepper, parsley to taste

Direction:

1. Clean the chicken and place it inside the basket previously greased with the cooking spray.

2. Set the temperature to 180 °C and cook the chicken pieces for 15 minutes.
3. Add the celery mince, carrots, onions, garlic, red wine, salt, pepper, and simmer for an additional 5 minutes.
4. Then pour the tomato and olives and finish simmering for additional 20 minutes stirring chicken and sauce.
5. Once cooked, add a handful of chopped parsley, and serve hot with mash or polenta.

Nutrition:

Calories 233, Fat 7g, 10g carbohydrates, Sugars 2.2g, Protein 34.7g, Cholesterol 98.5mg

Sweet Sriracha Turkey Legs

Preparation Time: 10 minutes

Cooking Time: 35 minutes

Servings: 2

Ingredients:
- 1-pound turkey legs
- 1 tablespoon butter
- 1 tablespoon cilantro
- 1 tablespoon chives
- 1 tablespoon scallions
- 4 tablespoons sriracha sauce
- 1½ tablespoons soy sauce
- ½ lime, juiced

Directions:
1. Preheat the Air fryer on Roasting mode to 360 degrees F for 3 minutes and grease an Air fryer basket.
2. Arrange the turkey legs in the Air fryer basket and cook for about 30 minutes, flipping several

times in between.

3. Mix butter, scallions, sriracha sauce, soy sauce and lime juice in the saucepan and cook for about for 3 minutes until the sauce thickens.
4. Drizzle this sauce over the turkey legs and garnish with cilantro and chives to serve.

Nutrition:

Calories: 361, Fat: 16.3g, Carbohydrates: 9.3g, Sugar: 18.2g, Protein: 33.3g, Sodium: 515mg

Turkey with Fig Sauce

Preparation Time: 40 minutes

Servings: 4

Ingredients:

- 2 turkey breasts; halved
- 1 shallot; chopped.
- 1/2 cup red wine
- 1 cup chicken stock
- 1 tbsp. olive oil
- 3 tbsp. butter; melted
- 1/2 tsp. garlic powder
- 1 tbsp. white flour
- 1/4 tsp. sweet paprika
- 4 tbsp. figs; chopped.
- Salt and black pepper to taste

Directions:

1. Heat up a pan with olive oil and 1½ tbsp. of the butter over medium-high heat.

2. Add the shallots, stir and cook for 2 minutes
3. Add the garlic powder, paprika, stock, salt, pepper, wine and the figs; stir and cook for 7-8 minutes.
4. Next, add the flour, stir well and cook the sauce for 1-2 minutes more; take off heat
5. Season the turkey with salt and pepper and drizzle the remaining 1½ tbsp. of butter over them
6. Place the turkey in your air fryer's basket and cook at 380°F for 15 minutes, flipping them halfway. Divide between plates, drizzle the sauce all over and serve.

Chicken and Chickpeas

Preparation Time: 35 minutes

Servings: 4

Ingredients:

- 2 lbs. chicken thighs; boneless
- 5 oz. bacon; cooked and crumbled
- 8 oz. canned chickpeas; drained
- 1 cup chicken stock
- 1 tsp. balsamic v*inegar
- 1 cup yellow onion; chopped.
- 2 tbsp. olive oil
- 2 carrots; chopped.
- 1 tbsp. parsley; chopped.
- Salt and black pepper to taste

Directions:

1. Heat up a pan that fits your air fryer with the oil over medium heat.

2. Add the onions, carrots, salt and pepper; stir and sauté for 3-4 minutes.
3. Add the chicken, stock, vinegar and chickpeas; then toss
4. Place the pan in the fryer and cook at 380 °F for 20 minutes
5. Add the bacon and the parsley and toss again. Divide everything between plates and serve.

Cumin Chicken Wings

Preparation Time: 10 minutes

Cooking Time: 31 minutes

Serve: 6

Ingredients:

- 12 chicken wings
- 2 tsp cumin seeds
- 1/2 tsp turmeric
- 1 garlic clove, minced
- 3 tbsp ghee
- 1/2 tsp pepper
- 1/2 tsp salt

Directions:

1. Preheat the air fryer to 400 °F.
2. In a large bowl, mix together 1 teaspoon cumin, 1 tbsp ghee, turmeric, pepper, and salt.
3. Add chicken wings to the bowl and toss until well coated.

4. Add chicken wings into the air fryer basket and cook for 24 minutes. Shake basket halfway through.
5. Turn chicken wings to another side and cook for 5 minutes more.
6. Meanwhile, heat remaining ghee in a pan over medium heat.
7. Once the ghee is melted add garlic and cumin and cook for a minute. Remove pan from heat and set aside.
8. Remove chicken wings from air fryer and spoon ghee mixture over each chicken wing.
9. Cook chicken wings 2-3 minutes more.
10. Serve and enjoy.

Nutrition:

Calories 375, Fat 27.9 g, Carbohydrates 11 g, Sugar 0 g, Protein 19 g, Cholesterol 94 mg

Chicken Sandwich

Cooking Time: 16 minutes

Servings: 2

Ingredients:

- 2 chicken breasts; boneless and skinless
- 4 hamburger buns; buttered or toasted
- 2 eggs
- 8 dill pickle chips
- 1/2 cup dill pickle juice
- 1 cup all-purpose flour
- 1/2 cup milk
- 2 tbsp. powdered sugar
- 1 tsp. paprika
- 1 tsp. sea salt
- 1/2 tsp. ground black pepper
- 1/2 tsp. garlic powder
- 1/4 tsp. ground celery seed
- 1 tbsp. extra-virgin olive oil

Directions:

1. Place chicken in a Ziploc bag and pound into ½ inch thickness. Then, depending on its size, cut chicken into 2-3 pieces
2. Return chicken to Ziploc bag and pour in pickle juice. Marinate for at least 30 minutes in the refrigerator.
3. In a bowl, beat the eggs together with the milk. Then, in another bowl, combine the flour with the sugar and spices.
4. Using tongs, coat the chicken with the egg mixture first, then with the flour mixture. Shake off the excess.
5. Spray the bottom of the air fryer with olive oil and add the chicken. Spray the chicken with oil as well and cook at 340 °F for 6 minutes
6. Flip over the chicken and spray with oil again, then cook for another 6 minutes.
7. Raise the temperature to 400 °F and cook for 2 minutes on each side. Then, serve on buttered and toasted buns along with the pickle chips.

Herbed Pork Burgers

Preparation Time: 15 minutes

Cooking Time: 45 minutes

Servings: 8

Ingredients:

- 21-ounce ground pork
- 2 small onions, chopped
- 8 burger buns
- 2 teaspoons fresh basil, chopped
- ½ cup cheddar cheese, grated
- 2 teaspoons mustard
- 2 teaspoons garlic puree
- 2 teaspoons tomato puree
- Salt and freshly ground black pepper, to taste
- 2 teaspoons dried mixed herbs, crushed

Directions:

1. Preheat the Air fryer to 395 °F and grease an Air fryer basket.

2. Mix all the ingredients in a bowl except cheese and buns.
3. Make 8 equal-sized patties from the pork mixture and arrange thee patties in the Air fryer basket.
4. Cook for about 45 minutes, flipping once in between and arrange the patties in buns with cheese to serve.

Nutrition:

Calories: 289, Fat: 6.5g, Carbohydrates: 29.2g, Sugar: 4.9g, Protein: 28.7g, Sodium: 384mg

Garlic Butter Pork Chops

Preparation Time: 10 minutes

Cooking Time: 8 minutes

Servings: 4

Ingredients:

- 4 pork chops
- 2 teaspoons parsley
- 1 tablespoon coconut butter
- 1 tablespoon coconut oil
- 2 teaspoons garlic, grated
- Salt and black pepper, to taste

Directions:

1. Preheat the Air fryer to 350 degrees F and grease an Air fryer basket.
2. Mix all the seasonings, coconut oil, garlic, butter, and parsley in a bowl and coat the pork chops with it.
3. Cover the chops with foil and refrigerate to marinate for about 1 hour.

4. Remove the foil and arrange the chops in the Air fryer basket.
5. Cook for about 8 minutes and dish out in a bowl to serve warm.

Nutrition:

Calories: 311, Fat: 25.5g, Carbohydrates: 1.4g, Sugar: 0.3g, Protein: 18.4g, Sodium: 58mg

Jalapeno Beef

Preparation Time: 45 minutes

Servings: 6

Ingredients:

- 1½ lbs. ground beef
- 20 oz. canned tomatoes; chopped.
- 16 oz. canned white beans; drained
- 1 cup beef stock

- 3 tbsp. chili powder
- 2 tbsp. olive oil
- 6 garlic cloves; chopped.
- 1 red onion; chopped.
- 7 jalapeno peppers; diced
- Salt and black pepper to taste

Directions:

1. Heat up the oil in a pan that fits your air fryer over medium heat.
2. Add the beef and the onions, stir and cook for 2 minutes
3. Add all remaining ingredients and stir; cook for 3 minutes more
4. Place the pan in the air fryer and cook at 380°F for 35 minutes. Divide everything into bowls and serve.

Marinated Beef

Preparation Time: 30 minutes

Servings: 4

Ingredients:

- 3 lbs. chuck roast; cut into thin strips
- 1/2 cup black soy sauce
- 1/2 cup soy sauce
- 3 red peppers; dried and crushed
- 1 tbsp. olive oil
- 5 garlic cloves; minced
- 2 tbsp. fish sauce

Directions:

1. In a bowl, combine the beef with all ingredients; toss well and place in the fridge for 10 minutes.
2. Transfer the beef to your air fryer's basket and cook at 380 °F for 20 minutes. Serve with a side salad

Roast Pork with Vegetables

Preparation time: 20 minutes,

Cooking time: more than 60 minutes;

Serve: 8

Ingredients

- 1 kg of pork loin
- 3 potatoes
- 4 carrots

- 1 onion
- 1 clove garlic
- 250 ml broth
- Salt and pepper to taste

Directions:

1. Place the tenderloin in the center of the tank, as well as the vegetables in small pieces, salt, pepper and pour a little broth.
2. Set the temperature to 160 ^{0}C. Simmer for 1 hour and 30 minutes. Mix the vegetables occasionally and turn the loin halfway through cooking. Add some broth as necessary to keep the meat tender.

Nutrition:

Calories 487.3, Fat 16.7 g, Carbohydrate 40.3 g, Sugars 1.1 g, Protein 44.9 g, Cholesterol 95.3 mg

Almond Asparagus

Preparation Time: 21 minutes

Servings: 3

Ingredients:

- 1 lb. asparagus
- 2 tbsp. balsamic vinegar
- 1/3 cup almonds, sliced
- 2 tbsp. olive oil

- Salt and ground black pepper; as your liking

Directions:

1. In a bowl; mix together the asparagus, oil, vinegar, salt and black pepper. Set the temperature of air fryer to 400 °F. Grease an air fryer basket.
2. Arrange asparagus into the prepared air fryer basket in a single layer and top with the almond slices.
3. Air fry for about 5 to 6 minutes.
4. Remove from air fryer and transfer the asparagus onto serving plates. Serve hot.

Crispy Marinated Tofu

Preparation Time: 35 minutes

Servings: 3

Ingredients:

- 1: 14-oz block firm tofu, pressed and cut into 1-inch cubes
- 1 tbsp. cornstarch
- 2 tbsp. low sodium soy sauce
- 1 tsp. seasoned rice vinegar
- 2 tsp. sesame oil; toasted

Directions:

1. In a bowl mix well tofu, soy sauce, sesame oil and vinegar. Set aside to marinate for about 25 to 30 minutes. Coat the tofu cubes evenly with cornstarch.
2. Set the temperature of air fryer to 370°F. Grease an air fryer basket. Arrange tofu pieces into the prepared air fryer basket in a single layer.
3. Air fry for about 20 minutes, shaking once halfway through.
4. Remove from air fryer and transfer the tofu onto serving plates. Serve warm.

Lemon Rice Soup

Preparation Time: 10 minutes

Cooking Time: 25 minutes

Servings: 6

Ingredients:

- ¾ cup lengthy grain rice
- 1 cup carrots, chopped
- 6 cups vegetable broth
- 1 cup onions, sliced
- ¾ cup lemon juice, freshly squeezed
- 3 teaspoons minced garlic
- 1 cup celery, chopped
- 2 tablespoons olive oil
- 2 tablespoons all-purpose flour
- Salt and pepper, to taste

Directions:

1. Put the oil, garlic, celery and onions in the Air fryer and select "Sauté".

2. Sauté for 4 minutes and add the rest of the ingredients except all-purpose flour and lemon juice.
3. Set the Air fryer to "Soup" and cook for 12 minutes at high pressure.
4. Release the pressure naturally and add the whisked lemon juice+ all-purpose flour mixture.
5. Let it simmer till the soup becomes thick and season with salt and pepper.

Nutrition:

Calories: 225; Total Fat: 12g; Carbs: 25.5g; Sugars: 4.9g; Protein: 5.1g

Coconut Lime Soup

Preparation Time: 6 minutes

Cooking Time: 10 minutes

Servings: 3-4

Ingredients:

- ½ Tbsp of coconut Oil
- 1 Teaspoon of ground coriander powder
- 1 Finely chopped onion
- 1 Medium sized Cauliflower that are broken into large floret
- 3 Cups of Vegetable Broth
- ½ Cup of Coconut Milk
- 2-3 Tbsp of Lime Juice
- 1 Pinch of Salt to taste

Directions:

1. Start by heating the Air fryer and set the Manual button to sauté mode and sauté the onion for 6 minutes.

2. Add the coriander and keep stirring for a couple of minutes.
3. Add the rest of the ingredients; from the cauliflower, the vegetable broth and the coconut milk; then stir the ingredients to combine them.
4. Lock the lid and set the timer to 10 minutes.
5. Once the timer sets off press the button keep warm and release the pressure
6. Blend the ingredients with a blender until it becomes soft
7. Add the lime juice and adjust the salt to taste
8. Serve and enjoy your soup!

Nutrition:

Calories – 262.8 Protein – 22 g. Fat – 12.7 g. Carbs – 16 g.

Spiced Butternut Squash (Vegan)

Servings: 4

Preparation Time: 15 minutes

Cooking Time: 20 minutes

Ingredients

- 1 medium butternut squash, peeled, seeded and cut into chunk
- 1/8 teaspoon garlic powder
- 2 teaspoons cumin seeds
- 1/8 teaspoon chili flakes, crushed
- 1 tablespoon olive oil
- 2 tablespoons pine nuts
- 2 tablespoons fresh cilantro, chopped
- Salt and ground black pepper, as required

Directions:

1. Set the temperature of air fryer to 375 degrees F. Grease an air fryer basket.
2. In a bowl, mix together the squash, spices, and oil.

3. Arrange butternut squash chunks into the prepared fryer basket.
4. Air fry for about 20 minutes, flipping occasionally.
5. Remove from air fryer and transfer the squash chunks onto serving plates.
6. Garnish with pine nuts and cilantro.
7. Serve.

Nutrition:

Calories: 165, Carbohydrate: 27.6g, Protein: 3.1g, Fat: 6.9g, Sugar: 5.2g, Sodium: 50mg

Herbed Potatoes (Vegan)

Servings: 4

Preparation Time: 10 minutes

Cooking Time: 16 minutes

Ingredients

- 6 small potatoes, chopped
- 2 teaspoons mixed dried herbs
- 3 tablespoons olive oil

- 2 tablespoons fresh parsley, chopped
- Salt and ground black pepper, as required

Directions:

1. Set the temperature of air fryer to 356 degrees F. Grease an air fryer basket.
2. In a large bowl, add the potatoes, oil, herbs, salt and black pepper and toss to coat well.
3. Arrange the chopped potatoes into the prepared air fryer basket in a single layer.
4. Air fry for about 16 minutes, tossing once halfway through.
5. Remove from air fryer and transfer the potatoes onto serving plates.
6. Garnish with parsley and serve.

Nutrition:

Calories: 268, Carbohydrate: 40.4g, Protein: 4.4g, Fat: 10.8g, Sugar: 3g, Sodium: 55mg

Spicy Potatoes (Vegan)

Servings: 6

Preparation Time: 10 minutes

Cooking Time: 20 minutes

Ingredients

- 1¾ pounds waxy potatoes, peeled and cubed
- ½ teaspoon ground cumin
- ½ teaspoon ground coriander
- 1 tablespoon olive oil
- ½ teaspoon paprika
- Salt and freshly ground black pepper, as required

Directions:

1. In a large bowl of water, add the potatoes and set aside for about 30 minutes.
2. Drain the potatoes completely and dry with paper towels.
3. In a bowl, add the potatoes, oil, and spices and toss to coat well.

4. Set the temperature of air fryer to 355 degrees F. Grease an air fryer basket.
5. Arrange potato pieces into the prepared air fryer basket in a single layer.
6. Air fry for about 20 minutes.
7. Remove from air fryer and transfer the potato pieces onto serving plates.
8. Serve hot.

Nutrition:

Calories: 113, Carbohydrate: 21g, Protein: 2.3g, Fat: 2.5g, Sugar: 1.5g, Sodium: 35mg

Bow Tie Pasta Chips

Preparation Time: 10 minutes

Cooking Time: 10 minutes

Servings: 6

Ingredients:

- 2 cups white bow tie pasta
- 1 tablespoon olive oil
- 1 tablespoon nutritional yeast

- 1½ teaspoons Italian seasoning blend
- ½ teaspoon salt

Directions:

1. Cook the pasta for 1/2 the time called for on the package. Toss the drained pasta
2. with the olive oil or aquafaba, nutritional yeast, Italian seasoning, and salt.
3. Place about half of the mixture in your air fryer basket if yours is small; larger ones may be able to do cook in one batch.
4. Cook on 390 °F: 200 °C for 5 minutes. Shake the basket and cook 3 to 5 minutes more or until crunchy.

Nutrition:

Calories: 408, Fat: 23.1g, Carbohydrates: 52.6g, Sugar: 0g, Protein: 14.6g, Sodium: 688mg

Buttered Dinner Rolls

Preparation Time: 15 minutes

Cooking Time: 30 minutes

Servings: 12

Ingredients:

- 1 cup milk
- 3 cups plain flour
- 7½ tablespoons unsalted butter
- 1 tablespoon coconut oil
- 1 tablespoon olive oil
- 1 teaspoon yeast
- Salt and black pepper, to taste

Directions:

1. Preheat the Air fryer to 360 degree F and grease an Air fryer basket.
2. Put olive oil, milk and coconut oil in a pan and cook for about 3 minutes.
3. Remove from the heat and mix well.

4. Mix together plain flour, yeast, butter, salt and black pepper in a large bowl.
5. Knead well for about 5 minutes until a dough is formed.
6. Cover the dough with a damp cloth and keep aside for about 5 minutes in a warm place.
7. Knead the dough for about 5 minutes again with your hands.
8. Cover the dough with a damp cloth and keep aside for about 30 minutes in a warm place.
9. Divide the dough into 12 equal pieces and roll each into a ball.
10. Arrange 6 balls into the Air fryer basket in a single layer and cook for about 15 minutes.
11. Repeat with the remaining balls and serve warm.

Nutrition:

Calories: 208, Fat: 10.3g, Carbohydrates: 25g, Sugar: 1g, Protein: 4.1g, Sodium: 73mg

Baked Egg Plant with Bacon

Preparation Time: 15 minutes

Cooking Time: 35 minutes

Servings: 2

Ingredients:

- 2 egg plants, cut in half lengthwise
- ½ cup cheddar cheese, shredded
- ½ can: 7.5 oz. chili without beans
- 2 tablespoons cooked bacon bits
- Fresh scallions, thinly sliced
- 2 teaspoons kosher salt
- 2 tablespoons sour cream

Directions:

1. Preheat the Air fryer to 390 degree F and grease an Air fryer basket.
2. Place the egg plants with their skin side down in the Air fryer basket.
3. Cook for about 35 minutes and remove the egg plants from the Air fryer basket.

4. Top each half with salt, chili and cheddar cheese and transfer them back in the Air fryer basket.
5. Cook for 3 more minutes and dish out in a bowl.
6. Garnish with sour cream, bacon bits and scallions to serve.

Nutrition:

Calories: 548, Fat: 22.9g, Carbohydrates: 7.5g, Sugar: 10.9g, Protein: 40.1g, Sodium: 350mg

Walnut and Vanilla Bars

Preparation Time: 21 minutes

Servings: 4

Ingredients:

- 1 egg
- ¼ cup walnuts; chopped.
- ¼ cup almond flour
- 1/3 cup cocoa powder

- 7 tbsp. ghee; melted
- 3 tbsp. swerve
- ½ tsp. baking soda
- 1 tsp. vanilla extract

Directions:

1. Take a bowl and mix all the ingredients and stir well.
2. Spread this on a baking sheet that fits your air fryer lined with parchment paper.
3. Put it in the fryer and cook at 330 °F and bake for 16 minutes
4. Leave the bars to cool down, cut and serve

Nutrition:

Calories: 182; Fat: 12g; Fiber: 1g; Carbs: 3g; Protein: 6g

Currant Cookies

Preparation Time: 35 minutes

Servings: 6

Ingredients:

- ½ cup currants
- 2 cups almond flour
- ½ cup ghee; melted
- ½ cup swerve
- 1 tsp. vanilla extract

- 2 tsp. baking soda

Directions:

1. Take a bowl and mix all the ingredients and whisk well.
2. Spread this on a baking sheet lined with parchment paper, put the pan in the air fryer and cook at 350 °F for 30 minutes
3. Cool down; cut into rectangles and serve.

Nutrition:

Calories: 172; Fat: 5g; Fiber: 2g; Carbs: 3g; Protein: 5g

Fried Banana Slices

Preparation Time: 15 minutes

Cooking Time: 15 minutes

Servings: 8

Ingredients:

- 4 medium ripe bananas, peeled and cut in 4 pieces lengthwise
- 1/3 cup rice flour, divided
- 4 tablespoons corn flour
- 2 tablespoons desiccated coconut
- ½ teaspoon baking powder
- ½ teaspoon ground cardamom
- A pinch of salt

Directions:

1. Preheat the Air fryer to 390 degree F and grease an Air fryer basket.
2. Mix coconut, 2 tablespoons of rice flour, corn flour, baking powder, cardamom, and salt in a shallow bowl.

3. Stir in the water gradually and mix until a smooth mixture is formed.
4. Place the remaining rice flour in a second bowl and dip in the coconut mixture.
5. Dredge in the rice flour and arrange the banana slices into the Air fryer basket in a single layer.
6. Cook for about 15 minutes, flipping once in between and dish out onto plates to serve.

Nutrition:

Calories: 260, Fat: 6g, Carbohydrates: 51.2g, Sugar: 17.6g, Protein: 4.6g, Sodium: 49mg

Creamy Blackberry

Preparation Time: 18 minutes

Servings: 4

Ingredients:

- 1 cup blackberries
- 1/2 cup heavy cream
- 2 tsp. vanilla extract
- 5 tbsp. sugar
- 2 tsp. baking powder
- 1/2 cup butter; melted
- 2 eggs

Directions:

1. Place all of the ingredients in a bowl and whisk well.
2. Divide the mixture between 4 ramekins and place the ramekins in the fryer
3. Cook at 320 °F for 12 minutes. Refrigerate and serve cold

Pineapple and Carrot Cake

Preparation Time: 55 minutes

Servings: 6

Ingredients:

- 5 oz. flour
- 1/3 cup carrots; grated
- 1/4 cup pineapple juice
- 1/3 cup coconut flakes; shredded

- 1/2 cup sugar
- 3/4 tsp. baking powder
- 1/2 tsp. baking soda
- 1/2 tsp. cinnamon powder
- 1 egg; whisked
- 3 tbsp. yogurt
- 4 tbsp. vegetable oil
- Cooking spray

Directions:
1. Place all of the ingredients: except the cooking spray in a bowl and mix well.
2. Pour the mixture into a spring form pan, greased with cooking spray, that fits your air fryer
3. Place the pan in your air fryer and cook at 320 °F for 45 minutes. Allow the cake to cool before cutting and serving

Maple Cinnamon Buns

Servings: 9

Cooking Time: 30 minutes

Ingredients

- ¼ cup icing sugar
- ½ cup pecan nuts, toasted
- ¾ cup tablespoon unsweetened almond milk
- 1 ½ cup plain white flour, sifted
- 1 cup wholegrain flour, sifted
- 1 ½ tablespoon active yeast
- 1 tablespoon coconut oil, melted
- 2 ripe bananas, sliced
- 1 tablespoon ground flaxseed
- 2 teaspoons cinnamon powder
- 4 Medjool dates, pitted
- 4 tablespoons maple syrup

Directions:

1. Heat the ¾ cup almond milk to lukewarm and add the maple syrup and yeast. Allow the yeast to activate for 5 to 10 minutes.
2. Meanwhile, mix together flaxseed and 3 tablespoons of water to make the egg replacement. Allow flaxseed to soak for 2 minutes. Add the coconut oil.
3. Pour the flaxseed mixture to the yeast mixture.
4. In another bowl, combine the two types of flour and the 1 tablespoon cinnamon powder. Pour the yeast-flaxseed mixture and combine until dough forms.
5. Knead the dough on a floured surface for at least 10 minutes.
6. Place the kneaded dough in a greased bowl and cover with a kitchen towel. Leave in a warm and dark area for the bread to rise for 1 hour.
7. While the dough is rising, make the filling by mixing together the pecans, banana slices, and dates. Add 1 tablespoon of cinnamon powder.

8. Preheat the air fryer to 390 degree F.
9. Roll the risen dough on a floured surface until it is thin. Spread the pecan mixture on to the dough.
10. Roll the dough and cut into nine slices.
11. Place inside a dish that will fit in the air fryer and cook for 30 minutes.
12. Once cooked, sprinkle with icing sugar.

Nutrition:

Calories: 293; Carbohydrates: 44.9g; Protein: 5.6g; Fat:10.1 g

Bread Pudding with Cranberry

Servings: 4

Cooking Time: 45 minutes

Ingredients

- 1-1/2 cups milk
- 2-1/2 eggs
- 1/2 cup cranberries1 teaspoon butter
- 1/4 cup and 2 tablespoons white sugar
- 1/4 cup golden raisins
- 1/8 teaspoon ground cinnamon
- 3/4 cup heavy whipping cream
- 3/4 teaspoon lemon zest
- 3/4 teaspoon kosher salt
- 3/4 French baguettes, cut into 2-inch slices
- 3/8 vanilla bean, split and seeds scraped away

Directions:

1. Lightly grease baking pan of air fryer with cooking spray. Spread baguette slices, cranberries, and raisins.
2. In blender, blend well vanilla bean, cinnamon, salt, lemon zest, eggs, sugar, and cream. Pour over baguette slices. Let it soak for an hour.
3. Cover pan with foil.
4. For 35 minutes, cook on 330 °F.
5. Let it rest for 10 minutes.
6. Serve and enjoy.

Nutrition:

Calories: 581; Carbs: 76.1g; Protein: 15.8g; Fat: 23.7g

Notes

www.ingramcontent.com/pod-product-compliance
Lightning Source LLC
Chambersburg PA
CBHW070933080526
44589CB00013B/1498